STICKMEN'S GUIDE TO YOUR BRILLIANT BRAIN

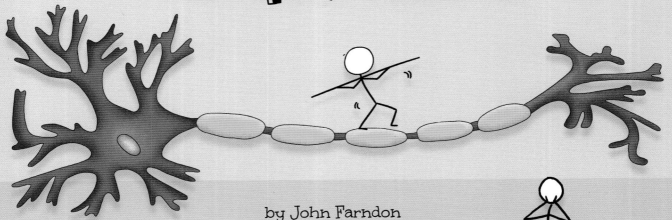

by John Farndon
Illustrated by Venitia Dean

HUNGRY TOMATO™

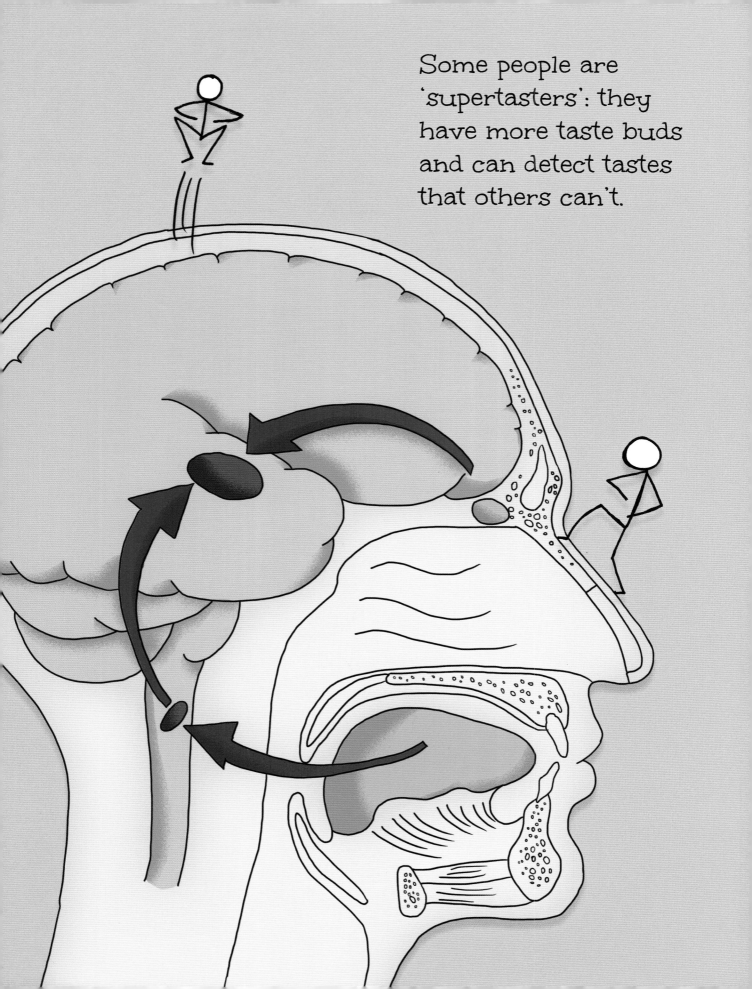

Some people are 'supertasters': they have more taste buds and can detect tastes that others can't.

Contents

Introduction

Every creature has a brain, but we humans have especially clever ones. The human brain is a living supercomputer! But like a computer, it needs inputs and outputs, and that's where nerves come in. Nerves provide input by sending signals to the brain from sensors all over the body, and output by sending signals to tell the body what to do. Your brain and nerves make up the nervous system.

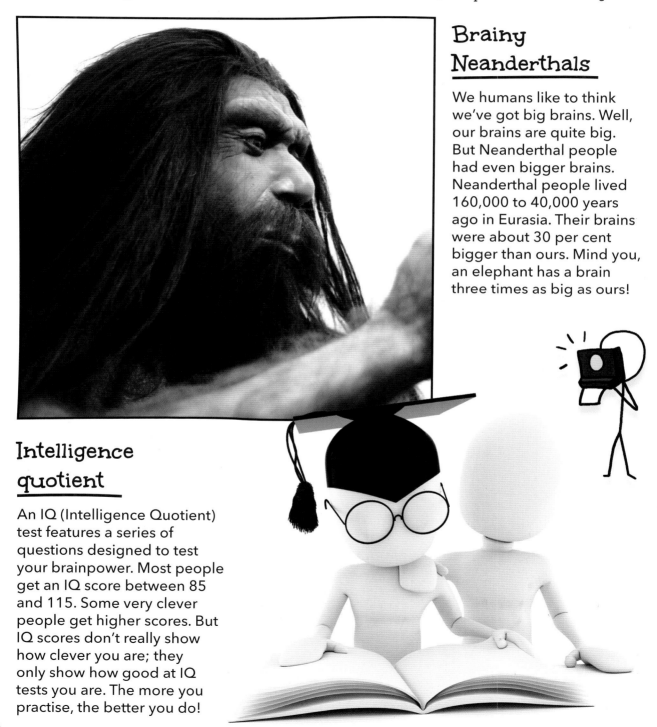

Brainy Neanderthals

We humans like to think we've got big brains. Well, our brains are quite big. But Neanderthal people had even bigger brains. Neanderthal people lived 160,000 to 40,000 years ago in Eurasia. Their brains were about 30 per cent bigger than ours. Mind you, an elephant has a brain three times as big as ours!

Intelligence quotient

An IQ (Intelligence Quotient) test features a series of questions designed to test your brainpower. Most people get an IQ score between 85 and 115. Some very clever people get higher scores. But IQ scores don't really show how clever you are; they only show how good at IQ tests you are. The more you practise, the better you do!

Just squidding

Most nerves are far too small to see, except under a powerful microscope. But the squid has a nerve with an axon (tail) that is over 1 mm thick – thicker than cotton thread. The axon sends the signal that fires the squid's jet propulsion system: the jet of water it shoots out to give it a quick burst of speed. Scientists have learned a lot about how our nerves work by studying the squid's giant nerve.

Mind your brain

Scientists and other thinkers often argue about whether you think with your brain or your mind. Your brain is the squidgy mass of nerves inside your head that does your thinking. Your mind is all your thoughts. If your brain were a computer, your mind would be all the things a computer does.

Sigmund Freud, the world's best-known psychologist

Brain science

Different sciences involve different aspects of the brain and how it works. Neuroscientists study how the brain and nerves work physically. Cognitive neuroscientists study how the nerves in your brain make you think. Psychologists study people's minds and how they behave, rather than their actual brains.

Central Control

Your nervous system is like a busy internet, wired to every part of your body, whizzing messages to and fro. It's a two-way system. Sensory nerves send signals in towards the brain, from sense receptors all around the body, such as the touch sensors in the skin. Motor nerves send signals in the other direction, out from the brain, telling the muscles to move.

Branching out

The core of the nervous system is the brain and the bundle of nerves running down through the backbone, known as the spinal cord. Together, the brain and spinal cord are known as the Central Nervous System (CNS), shown in green. From the CNS, nerves branch out to the whole body through what is called the Peripheral Nervous System (PNS), shown in pink. The main branches of the PNS are the 12 pairs of cranial nerves (in the brain) and the 31 pairs of spinal nerves. All other nerves branch off these.

Brain

Spinal cord

Intercostal nerves

Radial nerve in the back of the arm

Median nerve

Ulnar nerve

Femoral nerve

Tibial nerve at the back of the leg

Eight cervical nerves in the neck

12 thoracic nerves in the upper back

Five lumbar nerves in the lower back

Six sacral nerves at the base of the spine

Spinal cord

The spinal cord is the motorway that carries all nerve signals to and from the brain, and is protected inside a bath of 'cerebrospinal' fluid. The 31 pairs of major nerves that branch off the spinal cord form four groups: the cervical, thoracic, lumbar and sacral nerves.

Automatic nerves

Besides the CNS and PNS, you have a third system, the autonomic nervous system (ANS). This controls automatic tasks such as heartbeat and digestion. It has two parts: the 'parasympathetic', which deals with everyday tasks; and the 'sympathetic', which prepares your body for action if you are ever in danger.

Fight or Flight

The autonomic nervous system gets your body ready for action in times of danger, when you have to stand and fight or run away: the 'fight or flight' reflex.

The wandering nerve

The vagus nerve gets its name from the Latin for wandering – and that's just what it does. It wanders from the brain stem, all the way down from the base of your brain to the gut. On its way, it controls lots of things, from your breathing and heartbeat to the way you digest food.

Vagus nerve

Lung

Heart

Liver

Stomach

Kidney

Large intestine

Small intestine

Sciatic nerve

Sciatic nerve

The sciatic nerve is the largest single nerve in your body. It runs down from your lower spine into your buttocks and thighs, then all the way down to your feet. It plays a vital role in linking the spinal cord to the muscles in your legs and feet. It can sometimes cause a pain known as sciatica.

You've Got a Nerve

Your nervous system is made of lots of nerve cells strung together. Nerve cells, known as neurons, are unusual cells. While most cells are like little parcels, neurons are a spidery shape with threads branching out in all directions to connect with other nerves, or with sense organs or muscles.

A nerve cell

Nerve signals enter a neuron through any one of a bunch of spidery threads called dendrites. They then pass through the cell's nucleus and out the other side through a long tail or 'axon' to connect to other neurons. Axons from several cells bunch together like threads in a string to make nerve fibres.

Neuron

Dendrite

Cell body

Nucleus

How nerve signals move

Nerve signals are sent with a mix of chemistry and electricity. When a nerve is resting, there are lots of chemical ions (little particles) with 'negative' electricity on the inside. Nerve signals start by opening 'gates' in the nerve walls. This lets 'positive' sodium ions in. Positive ions like negative ions, so they are attracted towards the negative ions further up the nerve.

1. A nerve signal starts as gates open to let 'positive' sodium (Na) ions in

Positive ions are drawn to 'negative' ions further up the nerve

Segment of axon

2. The signal sweeps up the nerve, as more gates open further up to let sodium ions flood in

Other gates close behind the signal to let out 'positive' potassium (K) ions and keep the signal brief

Mind the gap

No two neurons ever touch because there is a tiny gap between them, called a synapse. When a nerve signal reaches a nerve end, tiny droplets of chemicals called neurotransmitters are released into the synapse. These chemicals lock onto matching receptor sites on the neighbouring cell, starting a new impulse.

Synapse

Dendrite

Axon

Neurotransmitters

Receptor site

Vesicle where neurotransmitters are stored

Axon

Myelin sleeve or 'sheath' providing insulation

Axon terminal

Love   Happiness   Depression

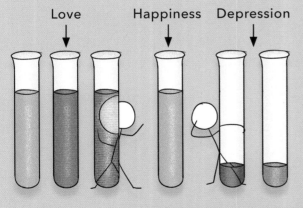

☐ Serotonin   ☐ Dopamine   ☐ Oxytocin

Mood makers

Different combinations of neurotransmitters have different effects on your mood. A lot of the neurotransmitter serotonin puts you in a good mood. Combine it with a lot of dopamine and oxytocin, and you're in love. The less serotonin and dopamine you have, the worse your mood.

Love it

When people first fall in love, their brains flood with dopamine, which makes them feel excited, energetic and focused. Perfect for dancing all night or talking for ages! But if they stay together and become affectionate, they get lots of oxytocin, too. This is triggered when you cuddle.

Brainy

Inside your head is an amazing computer: your brain. It is made from over 100 billion neurons, each connected to 10–20,000 other neurons. That means there are over a thousand trillion connections to help you think. No wonder you're so clever!

In your head

Your brain fills the inside of the top of your skull. The wrinkled outer layers are 'grey matter', which is pinkish-grey and made of the bodies of nerve cells, along with dendrites and synapses. The inside is mostly 'white matter' which is made of axons, the long tails of nerve cells.

If you're a girl, your brain weighs 2.5 per cent of your body weight, on average; if you're a boy, it weighs 2 per cent – but boys' brains are heavier on average.

A brain of two halves

Your brain is divided into two halves or hemispheres, linked by a huge bundle of nerves called the corpus callosum. Surprisingly, the left half of your brain controls the right side of your body, and the right half, your left side. Each side of your brain was once thought to have very different skills (as the picture shows), but many scientists now believe it is not so clearcut as this.

The Left Brain
The left side of the brain is good at logic, language, analytical thinking, numbers and reasoning.

Making your mind up

Your brain is actually 85 per cent water and quite a lot of fat. But what really matters is all the nerve cells, which are held in tight bundles by supporting cells called glial cells. All your thoughts come as signals whizzing this way and that through this amazing network.

Glial cell

Glial cell

Nerve cell

The Right Brain

The right side of the brain is best at expressing and reading emotions, recognizing faces, intuition, and creative tasks related to music, colour and images.

There's a thought!

Thoughts are nerve signals that buzz through the brain between nerve cells, making billions of connections in a fraction of a second. What you're thinking depends on which nerve pathways fire up. Pathways that are used a lot get stronger and quicker. Those that are little used tend to get lost.

Hungry brain!

All those cells in your brain need a lot of energy - and a lot of oxygen! If the blood supply to your brain were cut off, you'd lose consciousness in little more than 10 seconds, and die in minutes.

Inside Your Brain

The wrinkled outer layer of your brain is where conscious thoughts go on. Conscious thoughts are thoughts you know about. But there are other, subconscious thoughts occurring deep inside your brain that you know very little about!

Limbic system - smells, emotions and memories

Side view of brain

Cerebrum

Back of brain

Front of brain

Hypothalamus - how hot (and hot-tempered) you are

Thalamus relays signals to and from the brain; helps keep you awake or send you to sleep

Hippocampus - moods, learning and willpower

Amygdala - emotions and decision-making

Cerebellum - balance and coordination

Brainstem controls breathing and heart rate (without you knowing)

Inside and out

The outer layer of your brain is a dense mass of nerve cells. This is called the cerebrum and is where your conscious thoughts occur. The middle of your brain inside looks like a soggy mass, but there are other structures here, each with its own task.

On balance

For your body to make even a simple move, your brain has to issue precise controls to different muscles. It needs continual feedback from sensors in the muscles called proprioceptors, which tell you where every part of your body is. All these signals are coordinated in the cerebellum at the back of the brain, which then sends signals out to the correct muscles.

Brain base

The brainstem is the stalk at the base of your brain where it runs into your spine. It's the main pathway from your brain to the rest of your body, including your face and head. It controls your breathing and heart rate, and tells you when to go to sleep and when to eat.

Chess problem

When you play chess or similar games, you use the conscious part of your brain, the cerebral cortex, to figure out the problem. All the same, you get better with practice, as certain routines become established in your subconscious brain deep inside.

Seahorse brain

Right in the middle of your brain is a structure shaped like a seahorse. It's called the hippocampus, named after the Greek for 'horse' (hippo) and 'sea monster' (campus). It's linked with your moods, and is thought to play a key part in memory.

Hippocampus

Brain Map

The cerebrum is the large, walnut-shaped bit of your brain that wraps round the inner brain like a peach around its stone. The outside of this is called the cerebral cortex. This is where all the brain's clever activities go on. It receives messages from your senses and issues commands to your muscles.

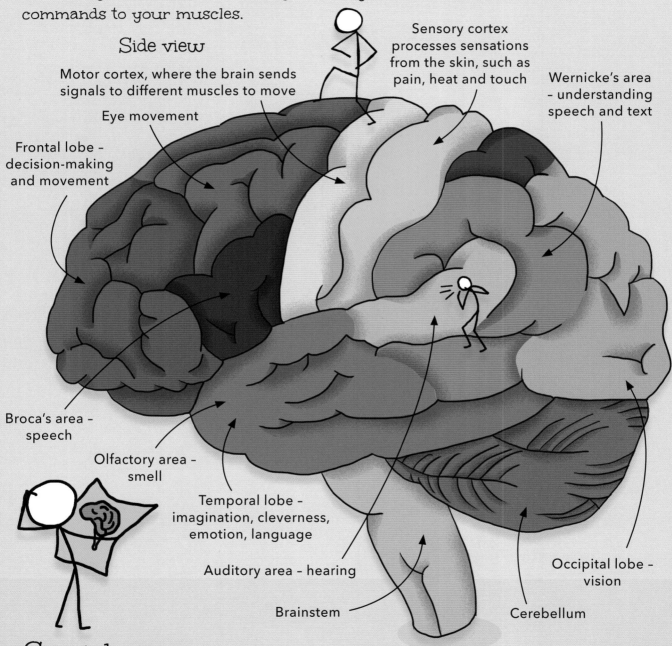

Side view

Motor cortex, where the brain sends signals to different muscles to move

Eye movement

Sensory cortex processes sensations from the skin, such as pain, heat and touch

Wernicke's area - understanding speech and text

Frontal lobe - decision-making and movement

Broca's area - speech

Olfactory area - smell

Temporal lobe - imagination, cleverness, emotion, language

Auditory area - hearing

Brainstem

Cerebellum

Occipital lobe - vision

Special areas

Each half of your brain has four ends, called lobes. A large, very prominent one at the front, called the frontal lobe, is where all your bright ideas happen. Lots of thoughts seem to take up the whole of your brain. Yet certain places in the brain, called association areas, seem to become especially active when you're doing certain things.

Top view
The left and right side of the cerebrum mirror each other

Frontal lobe

Motor cortex

Sensory cortex

Wernicke's area

Occipital lobe

The meaning spot

When you're reading, an area near the back of the brain called Wernicke's area seems to get excited. Wernicke's area seems to be the area where you work out what you're reading, and where you decide what you're going to say. It then sends instructions to Broca's area to work out how you say it.

Chatter spot

When you speak, an area of the brain near the front called Broca's area seems to be involved. Scientists are not quite sure how it works. They used to think that its role was just to put words together into proper sentences. Now they think it may help you understand what someone else is saying, too.

17

Moving and Feeling

There are two kinds of nerve that branch throughout your body away from your spine. 'Motor neurons' trigger muscles to make your body move. 'Sensory neurons' send signals from your senses to your brain to tell it what's going on.

Motor and sensory nerves are involved in whatever you're doing, whether it's writing a letter or playing football. Here's what happens when you're holding a pen:

1 Sensors in the tips of your finger and thumb trigger signals in the sensory nerve.

2 The signal travels to your spine and up to your brain.

3 In the brain, the signal is registered in the sensory cortex, a band running round the top of the brain, a bit like the strap on a set of headphones.

4 The brain responds in the neighbouring motor cortex to send out a signal.

5 The signal travels through the motor neuron back down through your spine.

6 The motor neuron triggers muscles in your hand to move your finger and thumb.

Feedback

Whenever you're doing something, such as playing electronic games, there is a non-stop interplay between sensory and motor nerves. The sensory nerves continually feed back data from the screen and from the world around you. The motor nerves in your hands control the screen.

Left side of the brain

A pain in the elbow

Whenever you suffer a sharp pain, such as a bang to your elbow, pain receptors send an alarm signal to your brain. You experience this alarm signal as pain. The pain is telling your body not to ignore the damage.

Reflexes

Reflexes are automatic reactions in your body over which you have no control. A reflex arc gives your body a way to respond to emergencies at lightning speed – before the danger signal has even reached your brain. It works like this:

7   You accidentally put your finger in a candle flame.

8   The sensory nerve from your finger at once sends a signal to your spine.

9   When the signal reaches your spine, it not only travels on to your brain, it also crosses through a link called an interneuron to the motor neuron.

10 The interneuron fires a signal down the motor neuron.

11 The motor neuron triggers the muscles in your arm to jerk your finger away from the flame super-quick.

Spinal cord

Seeing Things

Each of your eyes is an amazing camera with a powerful built-in lens that gives you an extraordinarily clear picture of the world. And behind your eyes, your brain has a clever visual processing system to make instant sense of the picture.

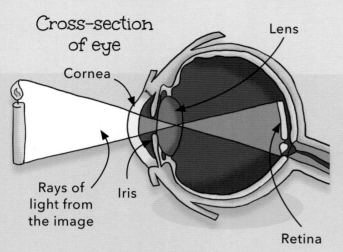

Cross-section of eye

Lens

Cornea

Rays of light from the image

Iris

Retina

Making a picture

Light from a scene you're looking at enters your eyes through the cornea, the main lens in the eye. This focuses the light to create a picture. The light then shines through a smaller lens that adjusts the focus to give a sharp picture, whether you are looking close-up or far away. The picture is upside-down but that doesn't bother your brain.

Red indicates left half of the scene. Blue indicates right half of the scene.

!?!

Pupil

Detail of retina

Cone

Retina

Optic nerve

Rod

Rods and cones

The lenses project the picture onto the back of the eye, known as the retina. Here, there are two kinds of light-sensitive cell to record the picture. There are 150 million rods that detect if it's dark or light, and they work even in very low light. And there are eight million cones that identify colours and work best in daylight.

Light or dark

Between the lenses, light passes through the pupil, the dark circle in the centre of your eyes. It looks black because your eye is dark inside. The coloured fringe around it is the iris. In bright light, tiny muscles in the iris constrict the pupil, making it small. In dim light, the iris opens the pupil wider to let in more light.

Pupil in bright light (above) and in dim light (right)

Your seeing brain

From the retina, signals zoom off to your brain down the optic nerve. The optic nerves from both eyes meet and cross at the optic chiasma. Here, the signals split: half from each eye go right and half go left, then travel to a sorting office called the LGN. The LGN analyses what kind of picture you're seeing - moving, strongly lined, dark, light and so on. It sends each aspect of the picture to the right place in your brain to be interpreted. Finally, your brain sees the pictures, right way up, on the screens of its own cinema, the visual cortex.

Direction of light travelling to your eyes

Left eye

Right eye

Optic nerve

Optic chiasma

Right LGN

Red indicates left half of what you see

Left LGN

Blue indicates right half of what you see

Visual cortex

Hear, Hear

Sounds are just vibrations in the air, and your ears are clever devices for picking these vibrations up. The flaps of skin on the sides of your head that you call ears are just their entrances. They funnel in sounds to super-sensitive detectors deep inside your brain.

The three ossicles

Stirrup Anvil Hammer

Cochlea

Eardrum

Ear canal

Sound vibrates the eardrum, which rattles the ossicles

The three parts of your ears

The earflap and funnel into your head is the outer ear. Inside your head is the middle ear, where sound hits a taut wall of skin called the eardrum, shaking it rapidly. As the eardrum shakes, it rattles three tiny bones or ossicles. These in turn tap on a window in a curly, fluid-filled tube called the cochlea, which makes up the inner ear. The rattling creates waves in the cochlea fluid, which waggle minute hairs so that they send signals to the brain.

The vibrations from the ossicles create waves in the cochlea that are detected by special hairs

The ossicles make the vibrations shorter but more powerful

Loud or soft?

Some sounds are loud. Some are very quiet.
Loudness can be measured in decibels (dB),
the force of sound waves against the ear.
The louder the sound, the more decibels it is.

Chainsaw

110 dB

130 dB

Jet engine

95 dB

Lawnmower

80 dB

Alarm clock

60 dB

20 dB

Ticking watch

Chatter

Two ears

There's a reason you have two
ears. It helps you pinpoint the
distance and direction of sounds.
Ears are so sensitive that they can
hear the very slight difference in
the time that sounds take to reach
each one. Your brain analyses the
difference, and tells you where the
sound is coming from. With stereo
earphones, you can fool the brain
into thinking the sounds really are
coming from different places.

Smell That, Taste That

Your nose may not be as sensitive as a dog's, but it can identify more than 3,000 different chemicals from their vapour alone. And it can detect just a few tiny particles from among billions in the air. And by working with smell, your taste is pretty sensitive, too.

2 When a smell sensor detects its molecule, it buzzes a signal to the nose's smell reception area, the olfactory bulb

3 Each kind of sensor sends its message to a structure called a glomerulus

4 When a glomerulus is triggered, it sends a message to the brain

5 The brain identifies the smell from the messages it receives

1 Vapour molecules travel up the nose

What is smell?

Things smell because they give off a vapour. You can detect them when just a few vapour molecules drift up your nose to the top and reach hair-like smell sensors on a patch called the olfactory epithelium. There are 400 or so kinds of sensor, each on the lookout for its own favourite smell molecule.

Olfactory bulb

Taste signal sent to brain

What is taste?

Your tongue's chemical receptors are called taste buds. There are 10,000, located in tiny pits all over your tongue. The tiny bumps or papillae on your tongue show where they are. There are five kinds of taste bud, each sensitive to a different flavour. There are taste buds for salty, sweet, sour and bitter tastes. There are also buds for a savoury taste called umami, which is the strong taste you get from meaty dishes and soy sauce. People once thought the taste buds for each taste were in different parts of the tongue, but now it seems they are all evenly spread.

Papillae on the tongue, containing taste buds

6 In each taste bud there is a cluster of cells with tiny hairs on the end

Bitter   Salty   Sweet   Umami   Sour

7 Saliva containing the food taste washes over these hairs

8 If the taste is right for the bud, the hairs trigger sensor cells beneath to send a signal

Dog on the scent

If you ever catch a bad smell, thank goodness you don't have a dog's acute sense of smell. A dog has over 50 times as many smell receptors as humans, and an olfactory area in its brain 40 times as large (in proportion to its brain). That means a dog's nose is up to ten million times as sensitive as yours!

Remember, Remember

If anyone tells you you're forgetful, they're wrong! The human brain has a fantastic ability to remember. There are billions of neurons in your brain, each connecting with thousands of others. When you remember something, your brain makes a new pathway of nerve connections, called a memory trace. You forget only when connections weaken through lack of use.

Will it last?

Memories are stored in your brain in three stages:

1   In sensory memory, new data arrives through your senses, and your senses go on seeing, hearing or feeling something momentarily.

2   In short-term memory, the brain stores data just long enough to pass it on – like remembering a phone number while you key it in.

3   In long-term memory, your brain makes strong connections so you remember things for a long time

Get it into your head

Your brain stores long-term memories in two ways. 'Explicit' memories are tucked away in your head quickly, and you only need to experience them a few times to remember them. But 'implicit' memories only lodge when you go over them again and again, such as learning to play the piano or football. Memories like these are stored by making nerve connections throughout your body, not just in your brain.

What a moment!
Some explicit memories are 'episodic.' These are dramatic episodes, such as a memorable Christmas. You remember every sensation and may be able to recall them years later.

It's a fact
Facts such as the tallest mountain (Mount Everest) are called 'semantic' memories. Your brain seems to store these in the temporal lobe in the left of your brain.

Practice makes perfect
You teach your body skills and procedures, such as playing a musical instrument, by practising them, so that the correct nerve connections are slowly reinforced.

Sensory memory

Transferred

Short-term memory

Transferred

Long-term memory

Forgotten

Forgotten

Where memories are stored

Sensations and experiences arrive in the brain via what is called the limbic system, which sits right in the middle. From there, they are despatched to various parts of the brain for storage.

Your semantic memory of facts and figures is stored in the temporal lobe at the front left of your brain

The limbic system is your brain's memory arrival lounge

The wrinkly cortex stores all kinds of memories

The hippocampus makes sure dramatic episodes are sent off to various places in your cortex for remembering long-term

The cerebellum works on procedural memories – the coordination of physical skills that you build up through practice

27

The History of the Brain

For a long time, scientists knew surprisingly little about the brain and nerves. They weren't even sure that the brain does your thinking. But discoveries about electricity and the development of microscopes led to breakthroughs from the 1780s. Knowing about electricity helped scientists understand how nerves work. Microscopes helped them see actual nerves for the first time.

450 BCE

The Ancient Greek thinker Alcmaeon was one of the first to realize that the brain is where your thoughts occur. Most people at the time believed thoughts happened in your heart.

1871

A young Italian anatomist named Camillo Golgi found out how to see nerve cells clearly, by staining them with silver nitrate. He saw that they have a single long tail, or axon, and spindly branches, or dendrites, that spread out from the spider-like cell body.

200 BCE — **1400** — **1600**

200 CE

The Roman doctor Galen believed that muscles were controlled by the lower, tougher part of the brain, the cerebellum, whereas the softer top of the brain controlled the senses. He was not entirely wrong – the cerebellum does coordinate muscles.

1630

The French thinker René Descartes believed that the mind interacted with the brain through a point in the centre of the brain called the pineal gland.

1780

The Italian scientist Luigi Galvani conducted famous experiments to make frogs' legs twitch by wiring them up to batteries. He concluded, partially correctly, that nerves work electrically.

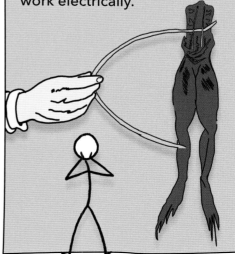

1890

The Spanish neuroscientist Santiago Ramón y Cajal discovered that nerve cells don't touch directly. Instead, they pass on signals across narrow gaps called synapses, in a kind of relay.

1906

The British neuroscientist Charles Sherrington showed that the nervous system is not one big single circuit, like an electrical circuit. It is lots of separate nerve cells working in balance.

1940s

The American scientists Edgar Adrian, Herbert Gasser and Joseph Erlanger showed that the electricity in a nerve is not like an electric current. Instead, it sweeps along the nerve as an 'action potential' – a difference in electrical charge between the inside of the nerve and the outside.

1800   1900   2000

1950

The American psychologist Karl Spencer Lashley experimented by testing how rats, with various bits of the brain removed, found their way through mazes. He concluded that memories are not stored in one place in the brain, but all through it.

1990s

The Swedish brain drug specialist Arvid Carlsson found that people with Parkinson's disease had low levels of the neurotransmitter, dopamine. This led to the development of L-DOPA, a drug for treating the disease.

1950s

The German scientist Bernard Katz and Austrian refugee Stephen Kuffler discovered that nerve signals are sent on to the next nerve across the synapse by means of special chemicals called neurotransmitters.

2001

The American neuroscientist Elkhonon Goldberg realized that brain activity is all coordinated by the brain's command centre right at the front, called the prefrontal cortex.

More Brainy Facts

Baby brain

Your brain grows at an amazing rate before you're born. At times, a quarter of a million neurons can be added every minute! But as soon as you're born, neurons stop growing and you have all the neurons you'll ever have.

Brain pruning

In fact, as you grow older, you lose more and more neurons in a process called apoptosis. That doesn't mean you become more stupid. It's actually a necessary process of streamlining, as unneeded neurons are weeded out. And the number of connections between neurons, the real key to cleverness, goes on growing and growing.

Growing brain

Even though you gain no more neurons after you're born, your brain continues to grow. By the time you're two, it's still only 80% of its adult size. So how is that? The answer is that the glial cells, the supporting cells around the neurons, continue to grow. Glial cells seem to protect your neurons and help them work better.

Mirror neurons

A few decades ago, scientists discovered that neurons don't fire just when you do something. Some neurons fire when someone else does something, too. These neurons are called mirror neurons. When you see a footballer weaving his way towards a goal, you feel involved because your own mirror neurons give you the same twisting and turning sensation.

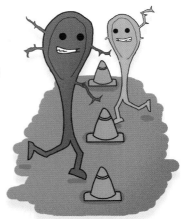

Hot head

Thinking is hard work. Your brain uses a lot of energy, more than any other part of the body. It uses more than 20 per cent of all your energy by itself. The brain runs on about 12 watts of power – about a fifth of the average electric light bulb.

A brain like Einstein

Girls' brains are slightly smaller than boys' brains, but it doesn't make them any less clever. The great scientist Albert Einstein had a smaller brain than average, yet he is thought to be one of the cleverest people ever.

Waste of space

Some people say you use only 10 per cent of your brain at any one time. A recent Hollywood movie was based on the idea that if you learned to use all your brain, you would gain superpowers. But it's a myth. All of your brain is already active all of the time, even when you're asleep.

INDEX

The Author

John Farndon is Royal Literary Fellow at City&Guilds in London, UK, and the author of a huge number of books for adults and children on science, technology and nature, including such international best-sellers as *Do Not Open* and *Do You Think You're Clever?* He has been shortlisted six times for the Royal Society's Young People's Book Prize for a science book, with titles such as *How the Earth Works, What Happens When?* and *Project Body* (2016).

The Illustrator

Venitia Dean is a freelance illustrator who grew up in Brighton, UK. She has always loved drawing ever since she could hold a pencil! As a teenager she discovered a passion for figurative illustration and when she turned 19 she was given a digital drawing tablet for her birthday and started transferring her work to the computer. She hasn't looked back since! As well as illustration, Venitia loves reading graphic novels, and walking her dog Peanut.

Picture Credits (abbreviations: t = top; b = bottom; c = centre; l = left; r = right)
© www.shutterstock.com:

6 tl, 6 br, 7 tl, 7 cr, 7 bl, 15 tl, 21 tr, 26 bl, 26 bc, 26 br,
7 bl = Tony Baggett / Shutterstock.com